Brunch for Mum

T0372149

Mum had slept in so
Dad and Sam were
cooking brunch for her.

Dad picked up the eggs but dropped one. It cracked and splattered on to the bench.

Dad slipped some eggs into
the pan to cook them.

"I'll get on to the crumpets," said Dad. Sam was concocting a drink for Mum.

Sam dropped chunks of
melon into the blender.

Then he added
plums and mint.

Sam pressed the little "on" button on the blender.

Liquid spilled out from the top! Sam had forgotten to put the lid back on!

Sam grabbed the lid and slammed it on. But there was a big mess on the bench. Sam moaned.

Then Dad said to Sam,
"I think I can smell burning."

"Crumpets!" yelled Sam.
Sam popped the crumpets
up and they were black.

"No problem," said Dad.
"I will fix up the mess.
You do the crumpets."

It was hectic for Sam
and Dad. There was a
lot of mess to sort out.

Then Mum sat down and
sipped on her drink and
munched on her eggs.

Mum said, "This is the best brunch ever! Thank you so much!" Then she added, "And you kept the mess down too!"

Words to blend

cooking	oops	cook
blender	ever	forgotten
for	spilled	black
bench	sort	moaned
burning	down	slept
splattered	smell	problem
drink	crumpets	munched

Before reading

Synopsis: Dad and Sam are going to give Mum a treat by cooking eggs on crumpets and making a melon drink for brunch.

Review graphemes/phonemes: oo er or oa ur ow

Story discussion: Look at the cover and read the title together. Ask: *What do you think Mum is going to have for brunch? Do you think she'll enjoy it?* Check that children know that brunch is a sort of late breakfast/early lunch.

Link to prior learning: Display a word with adjacent consonants from the story, e.g. *blender*. Ask children to put a dot under each single-letter grapheme (*b, l, e, n, d*) and a line under the digraph (*er*). Model, if necessary, how to sound out and blend the adjacent consonants together to read the word. Repeat with another word from the story, e.g. *problem*, and encourage children to sound out and blend the word independently.

Vocabulary check: concocting – mixing together different ingredients; hectic – very busy

Decoding practice: Display the word *splattered*. Focus on the *ed* at the end. Remind children that in some words these two letters make a /d/ sound at the end of the word. Sound out and blend all through the word: *s-p-l-a-tt-er-d*. Display the word *cracked* and ask children to practise reading it in the same way.

Tricky word practice: Display the word *was*. Read the word and ask children to show you the tricky bit (*a*, which makes the sound /o/). Practise reading and spelling the word.

After reading

Apply learning: Ask: *Were you surprised that Dad and Sam managed to cook the brunch well, and clear up the mess too? What did you think was going to happen in this story?*

Comprehension

- What did Sam and Dad make for Mum's brunch?
- What happened when Sam forgot to put the lid back on the blender?
- What did Mum think of the brunch, in the end?

Fluency

- Pick a page that most of the group read quite easily. Ask them to reread it with pace and expression. Model how to do this if necessary.
- Encourage children to read Dad's and Sam's words on pages 12 and 13, with lots of appropriate expression.
- Practise reading the words on page 17.

Tricky words review

so	her	into
said	he	out
they	do	there
were	one	some
said	little	put